Beauty Lessons

Beauty Lessons

by Terry Godbey

QUERCUS REVIEW PRESS
MODESTO, CA
2010

QUERCUS REVIEW POETRY SERIES
ANNUAL BOOK AWARD WINNER, 2009

Sam Pierstorff, *Editor*

Selection Committee:
Karen Baker, Ed Bearden, Cheryl Finley, Cleo Griffith, Jennifer Hamilton, Emily Malsam, Mark Nicoll-Johnson, Chad Sokolovsky, Gary Tomas, Gillian Wegner, Theron Westrope, Jason Wholstadter

Published by Quercus Review Press
English Department
Modesto Junior College
www.quercusreview.com

Cover design by Claire Zoghb

Printed on acid-free paper
10 9 8 7 6 5 4 3 2 1

ISBN 978-0-9743070-9-1
First Printing

Printed in the United States of America

for my son, Tyler,
whose name resonates throughout this book

Contents

Hunger

Who has not sat, afraid, before his own heart's curtain?

— Rainer Maria Rilke

Ready or Not

What Holds Me Up

My father runs behind me
down the alley, fingers hooked
under my bicycle seat.
Turning, I see he's dropped back,
nothing holds me up
but a fountain of air.
        Faith. Such foolishness.
                The ground flies up again.

Mike and Julie stand on their swings
to gawk. I'm entertainment
to be counted on,
like Captain Kangaroo with Cheerios,
fireflies in jars after dark.
Dad wipes my face, slick with shame,
        picks dirt
                from the pastry of my knee.

That night in a dream I circle the block,
wobbly then steadier, arms aching
from the clutch of handlebars, my ride so real
I awaken with hair wild from wind
and order my sleeping family
outdoors. Stunned, they do as I say,
shuffle in slippers onto the frosty grass.
They don't even yawn
as I climb on my blue bike
in panda pajamas
and glide away,
the simplest thing I've ever done,
the most spectacular,
clouds bandaging the sky
as I pedal past
one   two   five   ten
white houses with teetering porches.
        They will fall
                before I do.

Mittens

I hated
the red mittens you knitted me,
tried to hide
the simpleton string
that bound them,
balled my fists
against taunts of classmates
and longed
for grown-up gloves.

When no one was looking
I gnawed that vile cord in two,
teeth gritted, as determined
as the doctor who divided
mother and child,
both of us bellowing,

that first blood
spilling between us.

Combat

Saturday afternoons, the adults indoors
indulging in country songs and cocktails,
we'd gather outside
fresh off the latest episode of *Combat*
to fight over the biggest gun.

I was the only girl,
paid no attention to the tease
of popcorn and fudge,
just the pop and burn
of caps in my weapon,
pine-cone grenades,
tangle of bayberry bushes
as I ran and hid, shouted
and shot my friends,
my face camouflaged
in dried-mud makeup.
Hit a dozen times, I refused
to fall until someone insisted
"You're dead!"

How fortunate my mother's friends
bore no daughters.
I might have been stuck in my room,
enemy territory, dressing Barbie
for another date with Ken,
dragging out my dusty Dream House,
parting the curtain to watch the boys
and wanting to kill someone.

Lucy Fisher, Tetherball Queen

One minute I'm the new kid
slinking to the empty seat,
and the next, a kickball
smashes my cat-eye glasses
on the playground
and I'm whisked away.
Come morning
another grand entrance,
new glasses
and your eyes,
magnified by thick lenses,
bob before me.
You ask me to play at recess.
Tetherball.
No one dares laugh,
afraid of your steel wool stare,
your magic fist.

You and I are afraid, too,
afraid we'll never get past
pixie haircuts, overbites
and drooping knee socks,
but we don't talk about it, we play,
my head swiveling on its hinge
as you punch the ball
round and round.
I'm not tall
and you're a good eight inches shorter
but so relentless
I rarely sneak in a shot.

It doesn't matter that I never beat you,
that we aren't invited to jump rope,
that you must wear
the same two dresses day after day.
You are a quiet revolution,
teaching me to stare down fear,
showing me I will not break,
strength held tight in your fist,
your life spinning,
the knot holding.

Tremors

Our school desks always shook
as the Air Force test pilots
taking off from the dry lake beds
punched holes in the desert sky
and sewed them back together,
trailing white threads.

We had been told to take cover
under our desks
if we felt an earthquake
but no one ever budged.
Even when our books vibrated
the teachers never varied
their monotonous voices
for it was usually sleek aircraft
chasing away fear.

A big earthquake struck
as we all slept, killing 65 people
south of us, but simply rearranging
the neatly stacked homework
in our bedrooms. The aftershocks
shuddered daily and sonic booms
rattled the chalk in the classroom.
One day at lunch, a circle of us
looked up from the shrinking horizon
of our sandwiches
to see a blinding fireball.
There goes another test pilot, we said.

Two months later we gathered round
for the ceremony to rename our school
and the widow never needed a tissue.
She had known not to get too comfortable,
but this last transfer was final.
The sky and earth
would continue to quiver
and we learned the value
of staying in motion, of not listening
to the lull of complacency.

Shame

Mrs. Boyer's breasts swung
before me, escaping the V
of her mint-green dress,
nearly knocking my arithmetic lesson
off my desk. I tried not to stare.
"To make an 8, draw an S
and close the gate," she said,
guiding my hand, "like this."

At lunch I barely touched
my deviled-ham sandwich,
handed Jenny my cookie
without talk of a trade
then blundered through the wrong door
into the boys' bathroom
where Patrick stood
holding his sad stalk,
our mouths round in surprise.

When the bell sounded
I hurried home to my swing,
clutched the scratchy rope,
pumped hard, tried to kick
the laundry sagging on the line.
Six years old, and I'd never seen
a soul undressed,
had given little thought
to what we wore beneath our clothes
or why.

Over the fence, bells began to ring
at the church we never went to,
its steeple white and watchful,
and I knew it was God calling
to tell me I was a very bad girl
for looking,
for liking it.

Apples

Balanced on branches,
scraping our legs, we reached
for the imperfect fruit,
its pale, creamy peel almost pink,
devoured the sweet flesh,
twisted stems to confirm which boys
loved us best. We floated in air;
sunlight played in the lush lace
of leaves. Back then, nothing could equal
those scarred beauties, their ripe skin
and tang, ready to fall from the tree.
We longed to break away
from mothers who knew little of the world
beyond sewing patterns
and Campbell's soup cookbooks.
We dreamed of Brazil,
Rocky Mountain campfires,
roller coasters and conch shells,
dropped the chewed cores,
promised never to give ourselves over
to dull domestic chores, destined
to be among florid tarts waxed
and fitted for caramel costumes,
buttery beds of cinnamon and nutmeg,
a faint odor of rot
already rising from the grass.

Summers at Swan Lake

Sunlight poured from a genie's bottle,
painted the whirl of lanky limbs
scrambling for the water, the scumble

of rocks tipping us like sailboats,
the floating dock from which we dared
each other to leap, stunned, into the chill

and the motorboats whining like the bees
that always found our Popsicles.
Proud parasols of Queen Anne's lace

and raspberries fuzzy as worn toothbrushes
grew wild against our wilder plunder.
Ice cubes crackled in tall glasses

of cola, the lobster rolls and potato chips
never ran out, our swimsuits never quite dried
and we never admitted to being tired.

But at night the world fell away
like the day's clothes, leaving us
to our small cabin, its windows open,

our lumpy beds, the soothing sound
of shuffling cards. We dropped
like stones into the quiet lake

of dreams, the voices and laughter
of the grown-ups sweeping through
the sleeping rooms.

Beauty Lessons

Movie magazines stacked as tall
as teased hairdos, unlimited quarters
for Cokes and candy bars
and titillating talk wafting like perfume
suffused summer afternoons
in my aunt's beauty shop. In a lull,
a cousin would whisk me into her whirling chair,
twist my long hair onto hard rollers
and banish me to the kingdom of hot dryers,
sometimes brandishing eyebrow tweezers,
telling me *Ladies have to suffer for beauty.*
I looked around but there was no pain,
only the castanets of high heels,
the swishing of skirts, the gurgle
of a good time as the women in pink smocks
made gentle fun of husbands and children,
swapped recipes for casseroles
whipped up in avocado-colored kitchens
and passed on what Thelma said Erma
told Vivian over the backyard fence.
Talk often melted into laughter
or whispers, but strength and sex swirled
like clouds of Aqua Net
and cast a spell over the husbands
who poked their heads warily in the door
and jiggled their keys
but never entered.

First Bra

When I was 13
the lingerie department
sold only shame. My legs
thin as drinking straws
rooted me to the floor
as my mother sorted
through the boxes
like it was no big deal
and my father paced and grinned.
"Here's one your size,
38D," he teased. I shrank
even smaller
than 28AA.

Back home,
I was dwarfed by our neighbor Dotty,
her blouse straining to contain
lavish, wobbling breasts,
buttons near bursting,
bodice as overstuffed
as the couch where she sat
with my mother and sipped cream
and sugar with a little coffee.
One day I overheard Dad
tell Mom, "If that woman ever falls
down, we'll have to milk her
to get her up again."
Whenever she visited,
I averted my eyes,
escaped from the room.
I couldn't help but imagine
buckets of milk,
foaming,
sloshing.

Fourteen

We were most smitten
the first days of summer,
stretched out on our blankets
like the three months before us,
skin shimmering with coconut concoctions,
leaving greasy prints on *Seventeen* models.
Boys patrolled nearby, hoping to glimpse
the cocktail waitress
who answered the door in her bra
or waiting for long games of Twister,
faces so close, our bodies striking like matches.

Sticky and throbbing, we paraded to the pool
for its slap of icy water, me in my first bikini,
hot pink, with its hedge of chaste lace
my mother sewed on.
Only my breasts swam, the wet trim fallen,
boys holding their breath
and parting the water for close-ups,
their fish eyes red.

The sun slid down the sky's throat
like butterscotch, summoning us
to the street light for hide-and-seek.
Sam Hanson, star of my diary, shouted
I'm gonna kiss the last girl I find
and I ran, forgot about snakes and crouched,
pebbles tattooing my palms,
my breathing so loud
I feared it might give me away
too soon.

Gotcha.
The hairs on my arms stood up and cheered
and even with eyes closed I saw
what lay ahead, a tilting fun house
with boys behind every door
and no place to hide,
ready or not.

Bruise

I never could say no
to the night, mottled and blue
as the bruise on a plum, saved
my resistance for daytime's drone
of parents and teachers.

When he kissed me
under the street lamp,
our shadows accordioned
over the brown lawns.
A dozen girls lived inside me

like nesting dolls,
but he sugared his way
through plush red skirts,
cast aside painted hearts.
One by one the lights went out

in the windows, but we could see
everything we needed to.
The mottled mark
he left on my neck
darkened to plum.

Sweet Sixteen

I was carrying on about my milestone.
Next door, Rita was carrying on
with my best friend's father.

No one blamed her. Rita's husband,
Big Ralph, with flying saucer ears,
a chin that pooled like a doughnut,
never let Rita have any money.
She scrubbed floors at the base hospital,
took care of whiny Little Ralph,
owned exactly two housedresses, both plaid,
of discordant, spectacular hues.

I bounced out of bed on my birthday
to miniskirts and Stones records,
a reprieve from housework
and mushroom steak for dinner.
Mom and I left the dishes to soak,
joined Rita outdoors in the lawn chairs.
Terry's 16 years old today, my mother announced.

Big Ralph, greasy and bent over the hood
of his old Chevy, dragged over a webbed chair,
squeezed into it and pulled me onto his lap.
Sweet sixteen and never been kissed,
he shouted, whacking my bottom
with one meaty paw,
restraining me with the other.
Stop, I yelled.
STOP!
I slapped and kicked and glimpsed
through his thick, hairy ankles
the upside-down arrival of friends, neighbors.
I'm gonna spank you one time, he said, panting,
for ... every ... year!

I was sorry to be so old, sorrier still
to be so young. My mind spun
with wishes, and not the birthday-candle kind:
May the base commander rip the stripes
off your massive sleeves, may Little Ralph grow

to hate you as much as I do, may Rita's lovers
line the block. When he finished, I scrambled
to my feet, tried not to cry, snarled *That hurt!*
Aw, honey, he said, still smiling,
if that's the worst pain you ever know ...

Rita sighed.
My mother lit another cigarette.

Bad Girls

Waiting outside the liquor store,
we beg young GIs to buy us wine,
working them over with candy smiles
and hip-huggers so tight
they'd unzip if we sneezed.
"Be cool," they say, "we could lose our stripes
for this." We seize the brown-bagged magic
and thank them like good girls.

But we are bad girls,
passing the bottle before the game
and gagging on apple wine
till the delicious burn comes on.
Faces swim past
in the blur of stadium lights,
the popular boys pinball about the field.
They will strut into the party later
and we will be waiting
though we fear the advancing army
of hands, pity them their mighty urges.
We dance along the edge, and they wait
with nets held out in case we fall.
Secretly we want to jump
and they know it, especially the boys
who like us only a little, the boys
who drive fast cars.

"Hop in," one of them will shout,
but in the bumble of his affections
I'll think about the men
who sprang for our dizzy fun
and wonder how it would feel
to run a hand
over biceps the size of pool balls,
the mown lawns of buzz cuts.

Protestant

Growing up, I longed to be Catholic,
to dance my finger about my chest
and be carted off to catechism
like Danny Wagner, the boy I loved.
Or I could be Jewish with my dark hair
and chant words only we understood
and stomp on a glass at my wedding.
I wanted a church with candles,
songs that awakened souls,
sermons that roused my blood
from its stagnant pools,
to kneel and pray and feel
something. Years later I gave in
and took my grandmother to a Baptist church
where the minister ranted about indecency
and said women who wore bikinis
were headed straight to hell.
At home my skimpy suit
was dripping dry
so I mouthed "kiss my ass"
and told myself his problem
was he'd like to.
I would have stalked out
but my grandmother hummed softly
and the others nodded like dashboard dolls
— too old or too scared to have fun
or too ashamed to admit they wanted it —
but I decided then and there
that I wasn't
and goddamn it, I would have it.

One Can of Corn

We made it last three days,
parceling it out like change from a piggy bank.
It felt natural to be poor at 19,
my best friend and I proud of our sagging couch,
drunken three-legged table,
candle volcano in a Chianti bottle.
Fired from my typing job, I perfected my tan
while she swept sand from mildewed motel rooms
for pot and speed handed over by men
enamored of her cinnamon calves.
Evenings we'd set sail from clouds
of steam and White Shoulders
for ladies night's crush of free rum and Cokes
to stalk men with unscuffed shoes
and recent haircuts, stand-up guys
we'd lose later in the dance floor frenzy,
expectation melting from their faces.
We'd snag them with swaying hips,
tummies tight and brown as bongo drums,
and complain we'd forgotten dinner
till they begged to spoil us, ordering us drinks
with cherries impaled on swords,
baked potatoes dripping butter,
steaks that left red rings
on our plates.

Only Child

What It's Like

You wake each morning and hope
reality's the dream, surely your children
have not withered in your womb,
one after another.
Then you run your hand over your belly
and its flatness kicks you
back into your nightmare.

Not once
have you lasted
the first trimester.
Maybe this is payment
for the woman you used to be,
lapping up drinks and compliments,
getting everything you wanted, babies
the last thing on your mind.

Now they are the only thing.
All those shower invitations,
lame excuses,
gifts you have to buy anyway,
trudging through the graveyard
of the baby store.

Everyone but you
is having children, like it's easy,
but this is what you get: blood
in your underpants, cold blade
of the operating room, not quite
within earshot of the nursery
but you know they are there,

all those babies,
legs pedaling.

Hands

scrub
peel
stir
wash
cut
pour

Watch them wither
in the soapy sink
as you wait
for the mailman
the school bus
the clock
to announce
it's time
for that first drink.

You know it's not
about crumbs
and polished wood,
the cookies
the coffee
the man
you cram
into your body.

But it is.

Another deep blue dusk
and you miss it,
bent over a task,
bathed in fluorescence,
growing fat on drudgery.

Your capable hands
grasp skillets
scissors
spoons
but the days
slip through,
crack like eggs
onto the floor,
the one mess
you can't clean up.

Only Child: Blood

After I hobbled home from the hospital
with my fragile bundle, each encounter
with a stranger at the market or park

began with this thought: *You are here*
because a woman suffered unimaginably.
It was the only truth, louder

even than my son's fits of colic.
Those rare hours we slept, his pale face
rose as if from a pond and floated before me

till I rushed his crib to find him fine.
But I wasn't — unnerved and slow
to heal, lactation at full tilt

even on the graveyard shift,
those lonely hours,
the creamy moon our lamp.

Talk to him, his dad urged,
but I had yet to tap my cooing voice,
stayed silent through his slurps

and gurgles, worried I wasn't meant to be
a mother. I stayed in pajamas some days,
he underneath at his warm post,

safer than he'd ever be again,
though I didn't know it then.
I did what I could for him,

raised my blouse high, holding a place
for the words neither of us could yet say,
syllables soon to emblazon the air.

The Rivers in Maine

Some roll over the tongue,
loose and liquid,
Magalloway,
Salmon Falls,
Allagash.
Others are pebbles,
Passagassawakeag,
Megunticook,
Androscoggin,
more consonants
than my grandfather,
hoarder of words,
squandered in a day,
even when I left bits of shell
in his scrambled eggs.
After I cracked my head open
and he rushed me to Maine General
in his fire-chief car,
I hated to fracture
those pale faces,
bleed viscous yellow
into blue bowls.
Hardened by blizzards
and emergencies
but soft inside,
he forgave my breakfasts,
drove me every evening
in my pajamas for vanilla ice cream
just across the bridge,
the river flush with snowmelt
beneath our dripping cones.
Now I indulge my son,
show him how to break eggs
for cookies, nothing delicate
about his method, all sharp edges
and ooze – the shell mosaic
collapses with a crunch
and yolk cascades
through his fingers,
primitive and lush
as the rivers in Maine,
Swift, Mad,
Ducktrap,
Hardscrabble.

Basketball Coach

How I envy his
cropped wash-and-wear
hair he can shake
dry like a dog, his easy
uniform of T-shirt and baggy
shorts. Each morning,
10 minutes max and he's ready
for his work of play. *Hustle,*
he orders his small charges,
hustle, and he shows how
to break away, pivot, slip out
of the thicket of boys,
a knot coming untied.
He leaps, carved calves,
feet on fire,
sinking the orange sun,
again, again, again,
each release from his long
fingers a kind of bliss,
urging the ball to kiss the glass,
hands-in-the-cookie-jar pose
after each shot, every muscle
tense, each movement sprung
from instinct, the throb-throb-throb
of the ball, its crazy orbits,
the arc, the swish,
the net swinging
like a woman's skirt.

Almost There

"Are we almost there?"
asks my son on the way to the beach,
a birthday party, his grandparents'
house and yes, the emergency room,
a gash under his eye
from making like Tarzan
in his closet.

"Are we almost there?"
He must ask and can't bear
to be told, "No, 15 more minutes"
because minutes are hours,
hours are days, when a boy is 5.
He wants everything this instant
just as I once did, before I learned
I'd have to work for it,
suffer, pay for it. In 13 years
he will have reached
his destination, going to college
or living with a girl, phoning
on weekends out of duty,
but now he calls "Mom, Mom, Mom"
all day until I can't think.

"Are we almost there?"
Yes, because years are days,
months are minutes, when a woman is 44
and her only child
spins through the house like a top
heading for the door
and she knows that soon
she will have her quiet
and too much time
to think.

Where Grief Lives

His brain swells like a sea sponge,
red digits and beeps
counting down the hours.
Afraid to touch his body,
broken as a kite, my sister kisses
his hand, bigger than hers
but still that newborn fist.

She smoothes salve on his lips,
promises he will be okay
in case he can still hear,
plays on an endless loop
the moment she let him ride away,
shouted his book report was due,
spaghetti would be ready at six.

On the eleventh day he awakens,
a trauma nurse tells us,
and we can see him soon.
In relief, we weep with the wife
of the principal who fell from a ladder,
the cops whose buddy lost an eye to a bullet,
only to learn an hour later it was a mistake:
another boy had returned from the dead.

I cling to my sister's shaky scaffolding.
We sway and shout, refuse a room
to calm down in, stagger to his side.
She apologizes for not being a perfect mother,
reminds him of their Mojave sojourn,
thinks of all the places he'll never visit,
a bride not kissed, seventeen candles
that will stay in the box.

Perhaps her boy is watching
from somewhere else by now,
already gone from this room
where doctors hide behind clipboards,
organ stewards circle
and alarms are silenced
like children in church.

Hydrotherapy

I rinse away the boy-grit,
pile the sink with his chemistry lab
of green and purple bubble bath
and honey-colored shampoo,
plastic pirates with their beards of mildew.

It was my tub first.

Chamomile candle and Chardonnay
my playthings, books, paper, pen.
And quiet,
a drowning mother's raft.

The door creaks open just enough
to let my clouds escape, and he slips in,
defying orders to stay out, grinning,
as surprised as if he had caught me
coloring.

A shadow falls over his eyes.
You need a toy.
He plops a squirting frog onto the water
and sprays my book with droplets,
the president of one country
presenting the leader of another
with a treasured artifact.

I respect our cultural differences
and thank him.
The frog is more than a peace offering.
He is teaching me to be happy,
the one thing he can do better.

Eight Years Old

Even in winter, my son refuses to wear
a pajama top. When he comes near,
I lean close and brush his skin
or stroke it outright
like bolts of wedding satin,
and something catches in my throat
like undissolved chocolate
in a cup of cocoa. He is lush,
toes pink and curled
as the pearly hearts of seashells,
voice lifting and plunging,
a heron diving for fish,
his pogo-stick stride,
arms like clock hands gone wild,
the balloons of his cheeks when he grins,
and on his restless legs, faint hairs
pointing in all directions
as if ruffled by wind,
a great storm on the way.

Valentine's Day at Elementary School

Nora loves Tyler
who pointed her out to Brenner
who stared and stared
as if he'd died or something.
Now Brenner loves Nora
and gave her a special valentine
but Nora gave it back
with a message in code.
Tyler loves Nora
and Brenner
and the lollipop from Nora's card equally
and I wish I could assure my boy
love will always be merry and sweet,
but for every Nora
there will be three girls he loves
who don't love him
and for every Brenner
there will be three boys
pulling better snack cakes from their lunch boxes.
I want to tell him to treat girls
like candy wrapped in cellophane
and not get too close
because his heart is as thin
as the one made of red paper
he's clutching now
and I don't want it torn.
But I don't say any of that.
I say, "Are you hungry?
Would you like to go to the park?"

My Face at 46

I've seen enough of my mouth
wrinkled as a drawstring purse,
my parade of big teeth,
the two in front tipping forward
like drunks, my right ear higher
than the left, skewing my earrings
like weights on a grandfather clock.
God makes us like a puzzle
and sometimes he mixes up the pieces,
my little boy says. I don't blame anyone
but dread what's next: breasts slowly
letting go, hands speckled like trout.
Most mornings I figure why bother
and dash off without mascara
or lipstick. Is that really me,
or is it the young woman
out of a Flemish oil painting
I expect to see in the mirror, flesh firm
and unblemished, a touch of blush
from anticipation, the bowl of satiny fruit
bursting from the table
paling next to her untasted beauty,
her boundless appetites.

Hot Flashes

Here, I tell my son, get your clothes
out of the dryer
and your breakfast bowl and spoon
from the dishwasher.
Everything is clean. A *lady*
— I hear Jerry Lewis now —
cannot be expected
to put everything away, too,
can she, while dripping like a Popsicle?

"Mom, are you having flashbacks again?"

My estrogen is waving goodbye
along with my only child
but I clearly recall
tripping at a '70s Halloween party
where the costumes melted and changed
and changed again
right on people's bodies
and I couldn't tell what was real.
Was it safe to sit on a chair
or would I tumble to the floor
because it was imaginary?
So I stood,
waves of rainbows
and hummingbird wings
rolling around me.
I didn't know who I was
or what would be left
when the drug wore off,
maybe just a pile of clothes on the floor
with me gone.

Now I am melting again
and though I never liked the cold
I think of moving to Alaska
to roll in the snow like a dog,
my tongue hanging out.
I still don't know who I am,
a soothing cookie-mother
one moment, a ranting witch
the next, my nose long and bumpy,
my teeth black as my heart.

Only Child: Stone

Peek-a-boo baby has vanished –
the boy I tucked under my wing, flesh
from my flesh, bone from my bone,

my best magic trick, held up for the world's applause.
Gone are refrigerator-box spaceships,
hour-long ambles around the block,

sprawling, crayoned mornings
with no place we had to go.
I could not have foreseen

our voices raised so often in anger.
I learned childbirth
was not the worst kind of suffering.

We begin again each day, stroke
the velvet hours of possibility
till the quicksilver of misunderstanding

and we're at it again – flesh against flesh,
bone against bone: slapdash homework,
the heroin of computer games,

chores he will not do. He is not afraid
of my voice sharpened and brandished –
his bravado leaps and towers.

Stone against stone, we can't stop
scraping, can't stop drawing blood.
It may be all we have left.

Journey

Boats puncture the green cellophane
below, the fastest ones leaving
white crayoned smears
like you dashing through the house
in cartoon fashion, your life
streaking through mine.

I am descending over water,
feeling the same giddiness
as when you were born,
all nuzzling need,
and I was suspended,
not sure the ground
was still there. We floated
for weeks, sleepy and milk-spotted,
on the oasis of a rumpled bed.
The weight of your head
was stamped into the crook of my arm,
where today a carry-on presses,
pinching like your fingers once did
when I tried to pull away.

I was everything to you then,
the journey, the destination.
Now I'm almost home
but you'll be leaving soon,
pushing off with arms like oars,
growing small again.

Hunger

Two Mothers Stranded in the World

She circles, distraught and loud,
and like any expectant mother
displays an unfortunate waddle.
Behind her, a man emerges from the lake,
shoes and shins dripping,
holding her glistening oval
found on a lily pad
where it lay like a woman sunning.
He places it in the nest and she tests it gently
with her webbed foot, sits down
and settles in. Finally, explanation,
a boy had sailed the egg
into water two hours earlier.
The goose shuts her eyes, complete.
All around the air sighs with us,
and crape myrtle blossoms
fall feathery at our feet.
A woman breaks the silence:
"My son is going to Iraq.
We're pretty torn up about it,
but if the goose got her baby back,
that means I'll get mine back too,"
her voice thin as an eggshell,
and cracking.

My Grandmother Can See Her Husband's Grave From Her Front Door

Ninety-eight years is long enough.
I don't know what the good Lord
is waiting for.

I can't think what to say,
wanting to keep her with me,
bad knees and all,
though it feels as if she might crumble
in my embrace. I can't imagine
having my fill of life,
but she is ready for her next home,
her name carved on its smooth granite door,
next to my grandfather, as was her place.
She won't need her cane
or buzzer to call 911.
She has already paid someone
to pull the weeds.

> *I've been waiting 30 years*, he will say.
> *Why, I've thought of your fried chicken*
> *every single day.*
>
> *I got so tired of cooking for one*, she will reply.
> *I got so tired.*
>
> *Come here and lie beside me.*

And she will, like a woman
who has come to bed late
from doing chores
but knows she can sleep in.
Her gnarled limbs will unfurl like ribbons,
and she will pull up the loamy covers,
slipping, softly
as a breath, into silky slumber,
seeing in the dark.

Hunger

You could have become a farm wife
catching rainwater for her hair, a teacher
with crayoned tributes and shiny apples,
but in a tired café downtown
you droop over a stool,
cupping your chin in chapped hands.
The lunch crush over, you sink
into your break, slowly rounding the corner
of another afternoon.
Later you will sit at the window
in your olive chair,
a teacup warming your hands,
your parrot's hellos cascading,
lovely details for a painter
that do nothing to ease your craving.
Whatever happened to the boy
punished for carving your name in his desk,
the young man waving from the train,
his smile a cloud floating away from you,
the years of lovers not quite good enough?
Now the most you can hope for is contentment
settling like a cat at your feet
when you want a tiger, fistfuls of fur,
the smell of blood.
Watching the street lamp
layer the night, you can't help
but suck on regrets like peppermints.
No one to share the strawberries with,
to leave you silly notes, to take you away
from here. You know all about hunger,
waiting for the next customer,
waiting to throw down your apron
and get your hands good and dirty.

Bully

You lay in wait like a spider, Carol Hatchett,
came at me snarling after school, kicked
the air with your spindly legs, called me chicken.
I kept walking, my fear disguised as disgust,
arranged around me like a magician's cape.
Now I picture you dead, buckled
under the weight of your demons,
perhaps flattened like a cartoon character
under the wheels of a furniture truck
or struck by lightning
as you opened your umbrella at the bus stop,
finally learning what it feels like
to be singled out — your black eyes
staring at the sky, lashes shaggy
with mascara, dark puddles of quicksand
that consumed anyone who fell in.

Lust

I left home at 18,
lost my virginity one week later.
Couldn't wait to be rid of it,
like a dress my mother picked out
and forced me to wear.

All I remember:
his voice, small
as the rest of him, a ghost
of moon, watching.

I kicked that dress
to the back of the closet,
kicked him out,
began studying the braille of bodies.
Cocoa Beach was thick
with them, shipwrecked men
washing up at bars
to forget dead-end jobs.

Free drinks, as many as I wanted,
and the men who wanted me
made me giddy.
I was not beautiful
but men were easily fooled.
I couldn't get enough —
the hook of their stares,
bodies muscled and smooth,
the last of these
the man I would marry,
who lifted me, slippery as a fish,
from the water.

It's been decades
since I ground out that greedy woman
like a cigarette

but the names of old lovers
still roll off my tongue,
a stranger's lingering eyes
put me in mind of first times,
electric encounters when,
with hearts banging about in their cages,

we shucked
each other's clothes and shivered
at what we saw.

The gleaming, perfect flesh
of the catch,
impermanent, raw.

Produce Man

He lines up leaf lettuce,
tosses tomatoes past their time,
says he's fine, thanks,
until he looks in a mirror.
"When you're as ugly as I am
and you're from Alabama,
that's three strikes against you."
I don't question his math
but can't contradict him,
nose like a crookneck squash,
skin ruddy as a sweet potato,
a lonely fringe of hair in the back.
So we talk of the tropical storm,
he props broccoli
on their knobby legs
and I select bananas
still a little green
to ripen beside my window
where all afternoon
minestrone will steam
as rain sluices the glass.
He'll fuss over vegetables and fruit
only to watch them leave
in the arms of women
who never look at him
among the mangoes and artichokes
and find him appetizing,
this famished man
who feeds us all.

What David Told Me

it's impossible
to love just one woman
all of them so different
bodies like champagne flutes
mangoes   apricots
lush, searing skin
clipped, eager breaths
curve and sway
deep plush of their
kisses
dark spaces
and staggering light

what man could resist
what man would not sink into abundance
and risk everything he has

for what does he have
if he is not truly alive

if every cell
does not shiver and spark

what does he have

If I Were Her

If I were her I would stroke a candle flame
and not feel pain. I would thrum, steady

and silver as the rain. I would stride
with a heron's grace through thickets of night

jasmine. I would be a shovel cleaving stone,
a knife piercing the pomegranate,

a confetti of sand plinking
a sea-washed window.

I would ignite each silence and you
would not turn to another

with your confessions and your spit,
your threadbare stories. If I were her,

you would look at me
the way other men do

as if I were in a shop window
and you could neither afford to buy

nor leave empty-handed. You would stand
there and never walk away,

you simply could
not.

And the Neighbors Never Heard a Thing

He slips into the back row
ten minutes into my reading,
lurks in the second of silence
after the wrong number,
snaps the midnight bushes
as my key sticks in the lock.

Three decades
is not enough separation.

I still wonder why I let him in,
distant, older, full of excuses
why he was too good
for any job he could get,
a one-eyed, matted bear
I hoped to repair,
scarred from Cam Ranh Bay
where he covered the news
but didn't fight.
He came back home to do that.

I really don't remember his face
or that last argument,
only the broken bookshelf,
my nose knocked to one side,
streamers of blood,
his hot breath in my ear
and hiss of *When I'm done*
no man will want you,
the phone on the wall
swinging on its cord.

Snapshot

Still I see the four of us
wrapped in the mountain's shadow,
a horse the color of iced tea
eating from our hands.
Lucas shows off his new bride
and we wish their cottage
with its scrawl of chimney smoke
was ours. When my camera
swings out, it takes all of us
to wrench the sticky strap
from the horse's mouth.
He bares his sugar-cube teeth
for one last click
and we head indoors
to watch the fire devour perfect
loaves of wood.

One year later the horse is sold,
the pasture grown ragged,
and Lucas is gone
in an echoing shot
that stills every rocking chair
in the valley.
His wife learns the news at the diner
over lunch with her lover.
"She might as well have pulled
the trigger herself,"
an old man hisses.
The gallery of faces before her
fades like an old photograph,
the cold stones of their eyes
the last thing she sees
before she falls,
daylight snapping shut
like the afternoon she tumbled
into the river, but this time
she is not a little girl, this time
half a dozen men
will not jump in to save her.

Fear

At Rainier we were struck silent
when the mother and cub
rounded the corner on the trail
and pushed their quaking snouts toward us.
If we died, there would be something regal
about it, awe mixed with fear
at the great, swift paws, an immortal
story, not like other terrors —
        gasping and slapping away my oxygen mask,
        parrot screeches of the gurney wheels,
        the whites of my eyes rolling up.
We'd fight the bears if we had to
but there would be no point in groveling.
I would not have to hear again
        my watery voice begging the stranger
        Please don't, his knife lit up and flashing
        like a sign from God.
Much better to die in the forest,
to lie down in the roar and rich earth,
so much life tasted
in those open mouths.

Under Glass

All day it has rained,
clouds sliding defeated over eaves,
torrents rushing through streets,
and if you were beside me
I would tell you
about stomping through puddles
in little-girl galoshes
and the boys who chased me
to press hard-bodied
beetles against my wet face.

I would try to make you understand
how I squirmed to get away
though part of me wanted to stay,
the unnameable attraction kicking
inside me like a bug on its back,
the sinking that made me want
to lie down in the mud,
give myself over
to the nastiness of little boys
with eyes like bluebottle flies.

They stood over me
when I fell, laughed at my tears,
the blood where I bit my lip.
I was a specimen under glass,
they were taking notes.
Rain slipped under my slicker
till I was damp clear through,
and when they held down my arms
like you do sometimes
I fought them
and I didn't.

If you were here
I might warn you
I'm hard to scare away,
rain alone won't stop me.
Then again I might just smile,
say your name, roll it
around on my tongue,
eat you up,
spit you out.

Wilderness

Even as the wind
undresses the wildflowers
they welcome me, woman
with hair in disarray
like theirs.
Indian paintbrush,
lilies, lupine and trillium
nod indulgently
as I wade waist-deep
into scarlet, indigo and gold
recklessness.
The veil of bees
parts when you insist
on my snapshot
but I already know
I'll hate the photograph,
the unabashed blooms
diminishing me,
my grin rigid, unnatural.
Put away your camera
and touch me
here
and here.
This is how I want
to be remembered:
without any clothes,
without a smile,
just like this.

For This Life, We'll Be Serving Meat Loaf and Mashed Potatoes

Do you think you're the only one
ever plunged into the dark
on a long train ride?
Soon enough the lights blink back on,
new people settle into nearby seats:
a man staring past his newspaper,
a woman chewing red grapes and regret.
Look out the window.
It's the same old scrubbed-skillet sky,
raining on lovers and lonely alike.

Be patient. Your heart will stop
its slavish thumping
like the tail of a dog by the door.
Love almost always ends this way.

Watch the mountains
disappear past the window.
Summon the waiter
for meat loaf and mashed potatoes
and more than a little bourbon
to wash it all down.

You'd like to lie across the tracks
at the next station, but this is not
an old movie, there's no hero
to scoop you up. That nonsense
is what landed you here.
Hurry and pick yourself up
— it is enough right now
to eat and drink
and save your own life.

ACKNOWLEDGMENTS

Grateful acknowledgment is made to the editors of the following magazines and online journals in which many of these poems, sometimes in earlier versions, first appeared:

Artvoice: "Snapshot"
Aurorean: "Summers at Swan Lake"
The Café Review: "The Rivers in Maine"
CALYX Journal: "Where Grief Lives"
Connecticut Review: "Produce Man," "If I Were Her"
Dogwood: "Under Glass"
Florida Review: "What David Told Me"
Green Hills Literary Lantern: "Combat," "Basketball Coach," "Lust," "Fear"
Miller's Pond: "One Can of Corn"
Off the Coast: "Wilderness"
Passager: "Lucy Fisher, Tetherball Queen"
Pearl: "Shame," "Mittens"
Poet Lore: "Apples"
Potomac Review: "My Grandmother Can See Her Husband's Grave From Her Front Door," "Hunger," "Bad Girls"
Primavera: "Eight Years Old," "Journey"
Quercus Review: "Only Child"
Rattle: "My Face at 46"
Revelry: "Bully," "Protestant"
Rosebud: "Beauty Lessons"
Slipstream: "Sweet Sixteen," "Hands," "Hot Flashes," "Tremors," "First Bra," "Almost There"
Slow Trains Literary Journal: "For This Life, We'll Be Serving Meat Loaf and Mashed Potatoes," "What Holds Me Up"
Spillway: "What It's Like"
Yemassee: "Fourteen," "Hydrotherapy"

"Fourteen" also appeared in *Blue Arc West: An Anthology of California Poets*, Tebot Bach press.

"Mittens," "First Bra" and "Hot Flashes" also appeared in *Contrarywise: An Anthology*, Kings Estate Press.

"Eight Years Old" also appeared in *Unexpected Harvest: A Gathering of Blessings*, Kings Estate Press.

"Produce Man" was the winner of the 2008 Rita Dove Poetry Award.

"Mittens" was a winner of the 2007 Late Blooms Poetry Postcard Series contest.

Some of the poems in this collection were first published in the chapbook *Behind Every Door*, winner of Slipstream's 19th Annual Poetry Chapbook Contest (Slipstream Press, 2006).

"Where Grief Lives" is for Freddie Moseley.

I am grateful to Claire Zoghb, who read every word, pushed and supported me in equal measure, and designed this book's cover; to Susan Lilley, for her abundant insights, enthusiasm, home-cooked gourmet meals, wine, and affection; Lana Hechtman Ayers, who helped me shape my book; to Mary Glenn, who always believed in me; and to Philip F. Deaver, Suzannah Gilman, John Paul O'Connor, Caridad McCormick and Angelisa Pinkston Young for offering friendship, encouragement and valuable advice.

Many thanks also to Sam Pierstorff, for giving my poems a home; to Dorianne Laux, Billy Collins, Carolyn Forché, Nancy A. Henry and Dan Sicoli for their blessings and friendship; and to my family, who graciously puts up with my storytelling.

ABOUT THE AUTHOR

Terry Godbey has published more than 100 poems in *Rattle*, *Poet Lore*, *CALYX Journal*, *Pearl*, *The Café Review*, *Rosebud*, *Crab Creek Review*, *Harpur Palate*, *Connecticut Review* and other literary magazines. Her chapbook *Behind Every Door* won Slipstream's chapbook contest in 2006. She also won the 2008 Rita Dove Poetry Award and is a two-time Pushcart Prize nominee. She lives in Orlando with her son and works as a freelance writer and editor. This is her first full-length collection.

www.ingramcontent.com/pod-product-compliance
Lightning Source LLC
LaVergne TN
LVHW050943080826
845145LV00004B/1390

* 9 7 8 0 9 7 4 3 0 7 0 9 1 *